W9-CJX-305

THE POCKET LIBRARY OF GREAT ART

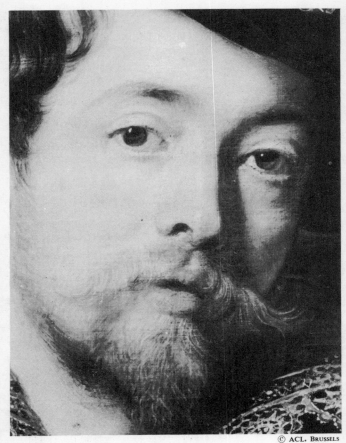

Plate 1. SELF-PORTRAIT (*detail of color plate 10*)

© ACL, BRUSSELS

PETER PAUL

RUBENS

(1577–1640)

text by

JULIUS S. HELD

Professor of Fine Arts, Barnard College
Columbia University, New York

published by HARRY N. ABRAMS, INC., *in association*
with POCKET BOOKS, INC., *New York*

On the cover
detail of SUSANNE FOURMENT (*plate 12*)

Copyright 1954 by Harry N. Abrams, Incorporated. Copyright in the United States and foreign countries under International Copyright Convention. All rights reserved under Pan-American Convention. No part of the contents of this book may be reproduced without the written permission of Harry N. Abrams, Incorporated. Printed in U.S.A. MILTON S. FOX, Editor

Plate 2. ST. GREGORY OF NAZIANZUS. *About 1620*
Oil sketch, 19¾ x 25¾". Albright Art Gallery, Buffalo

Pietro Pauolo Rubens

"And so they meet, the Ionian and the Fleming, the two greatest storytellers this old earth of ours has ever borne—Homer and Rubens."

With these words, Jacob Burckhardt, himself old and great, ended his last book, the printing of which he never saw. He had called it *Erinnerungen aus Rubens* (Recollections of Rubens)—grateful remembrances of over fifty years of friendship. Rubens, one might think, should have been the last artist to fascinate the author of *The Civilization of the Renaissance in Italy* and of other works on the culture of the Mediterranean world. By what magic, we may ask, did the sensuous Fleming charm the sober Swiss scholar of the nineteenth century? What hold had the most prominent artistic representative of the Catholic Counter-Reformation over the heir of Calvinist severity? What attractions were offered by the painter of Baroque exuberance to the classicist for whom the Greeks and their Italian pupils of the Renaissance had formulated the ideal of beauty once and for all?

Those who see in Rubens no more than a painter of amply proportioned women and swaggering men, or a facile decorator of immense spaces in Baroque palaces and churches, will never understand how the chasm between the two worlds could ever have been bridged. Only he who penetrates Rubens' world more deeply will find the answers to these questions. He will find that Rubens himself combined extremes in his own personality as well as in his art. He was a man of boundless vitality, yet at the same time used to strictest self-discipline. He moved with ease in the highest social circles, but he was also deeply attached to his Flemish earth and to the comforts of middle-class domesticity. He was a patriot who saw beyond the narrow limits of his own country, a statesman active in public affairs, yet at the same time a scholar thoroughly acquainted with the cultural traditions of the West.

His art, too, encompasses apparently opposite elements. For centuries he has been hailed as one of the greatest colorists, which he surely was; yet close study

© ACL, Brussels

Plate 3. MYSTIC MARRIAGE OF ST. CATHERINE. *About 1627–28*
18'6" x 13'1". Church of St. Augustine, Antwerp

Plate 4. VENUS AND ADONIS. *About* 1635. 77½ × 95¼".

The Metropolitan Museum of Art, New York. See detail, plate 20

shows that drawing—more exactly, line—played as important a role in Rubens' art as it did in that of Raphael. He had an incomparably vivid imagination which enabled him to sketch complicated forms and actions quickly; yet he also made studies from nature throughout his life with the same loving attention to texture and detail that for long had been the hallmark, the pride, and—in the judgment of some Italians—the limitation of Flemish art. Among his sources we find Hellenistic sculptures and Flemish primitives, Michelangelo's grand rhetoric and Caravaggio's naturalism, the sinuous bodies of the Mannerists, and the color-symphonies of the Venetians.

The range of Rubens' subject matter is equally wide. He did pictures of ancient gods and heroes who come to life not as pale shadows of philological pedantry, but as breathing, vibrant, warm-blooded human beings. There are saints who suffer the pains of martyrdom or who experience divine ecstasy, thoroughly credible in his painting no matter how strange their story. There are allegories in which scholastic personifications are built into real persons with emotional reactions common to all men. He painted portraits which give specific individuality to his models while at the same time making them typical representatives of their age, sex, or rank. Although primarily concerned with figures, human and animal, he contributed some of the finest works to the category of landscape painting, works in which an abundant earth is glorified and enveloped by the sun's warming light.

Thus, the discerning student of Rubens will find the master's work to be something very different from

Plate 5. Rubens and Frans Snyders. PROMETHEUS. *About 1616–18
95⅝ x 82½". Philadelphia Museum of Art (Wilstach Coll.)*

what it is assumed to be by popular conceptions, or misconceptions. There is bigness in Rubens, but also delicacy; strong action, but also sensitivity and lyricism. Burckhardt was right when he felt that it was a whole world that Rubens had created, and we might emphasize its *wholeness* as well as its scope. Within its enormous territory it is rich, full—and perfect. For also it has, of course, its boundaries, excluding those aspects which would disturb its perfection. The fragmentary, the irregular, the ugly had no place in it. The world of Rubens admits love and hate, exultation and suffering, life and death—but all of them whole, and with that kind of finality with which his figures are either children, or youths, or princes, or saints. It is a world of beauty in which beauty is a function of health and vitality.

There are other limitations, but—as with Homer— we do not seem to be aware of them as long as we stay within the orbit of the works themselves. Only from the outside, in the scrutiny of critical thought, do we detect the other possibilities: that Rembrandt knew of suffering deeper than any that Rubens thought of or projected; that the passing of time was caught in the quietude of Vermeer's canvases as persuasively as in the drama and commotion of Rubens' battle-scenes, or more so; that El Greco's weird shades and flickering light were more appropriate symbols for the interpretation of the visions of Catholic mystics than Rubens' cheerful colors.

No man can do everything. Rubens—like Titian— remains a "Painter of Kings, and a King of Painters," and we are grateful for the liberal gifts which he has showered upon us.

© ACL. BRUSSELS

Plate 6. DESIGN FOR CHARIOT FOR TRIUMPHAL PROCESSION AT ANTWERP
1638. Oil, 40½ x 28". Museum of Fine Arts, Antwerp

Plate 7. THOMAS HOWARD, EARL OF ARUNDEL. *About 1629–30*
Oil, 54 x 44⅞". Isabella Stewart Gardner Museum, Boston

Plate 8. PORTRAIT OF MULAY AHMED. *About 1610*
Oil, 39½ x 28". Museum of Fine Arts, Boston

© ACL, Brussels

Plate 9. SAMSON AND THE LION. *Design for a title page. 1634. Ink over black chalk, 7½ x 5¾". Plantin Moretus Museum, Antwerp*

COLOR PLATES

PLATE 10

RUBENS AND ISABELLA BRANT

Painted 1609/10. 70½ x 53½"
Neue Staatsgalerie, Munich

We see the young couple in the shade of a fragrant honeysuckle vine. Rubens, preceded by his fame abroad, had recently come home after eight years in Italy; his bride was the daughter of an influential and well-to-do Antwerp patrician. They make a decorous pair in their fashionable costumes braided, embroidered, buttoned, and adorned with lace. The artist, still in his early thirties, leans toward his young wife, who, sitting on the ground before him, lays her right hand trustingly on his in what looks like an accidental repetition of an age-old ceremonial gesture of marriage. Rubens' left hand lies relaxed on the hilt of his sword, but its index finger clearly points down at the joined hands, the nerve-center of the whole composition. The pair forms a union in which each partner remains an individual looking frankly at the beholder. The intimacy, the mutual trust, the tender love of the newlyweds are expressed by the smooth outline which ties the figures together, by the obvious parallelism and correspondence of their limbs, and by the harmonious interplay of the muted ochers, wine-reds, and dark greens.

PLATE II

THE ABDUCTION OF
THE DAUGHTERS OF LEUCIPPUS

Painted 1614–16. 87½ x 82¼"
Neue Staatsgalerie, Munich

Painted in figures larger than life on an almost square canvas, *The Abduction of the Daughters of Leucippus* seems at first primarily an exercise in composition. Four pairs of figures are combined into a single group that rises before us like an elaborate piece of sculpture. The eight bodies conform to a circular outline, and the weights and colors are so distributed that a balanced effect is achieved. Within this balance, there is a complicated use of counterpoise. One of the abductors is turning to the right, while his brother walks toward the left. One of the women is in mid-air, her body seen frontally and in a concave pose; her sister kneels on the ground, her back curving in the opposite direction. The sorrel horse moves toward the left foreground; the gray turns inward and rears.

Yet, no matter how calculated the balance nor how skillful the interweaving of movements, Rubens never lost sight of the fact that this is a story of love, and that abduction is one of the primeval marriage rites. The resistance of the maidens is but a token one. Thus the painting is less one of violence than of passion, less of fear than of modesty, and the equilibrium of the design corresponds legitimately to a basic feeling of harmony.

PLATE 12

SUSANNE FOURMENT
("LE CHAPEAU DE PAILLE")

Painted about 1622. 30¼ x 21"
National Gallery, London

The most puzzling thing about this picture has always
been its name, *Chapeau de Paille*. In modern usage
paille means straw, while the hat in the painting is evi-
dently of felt. Recently, however, it has been pointed out
that *paille* once had also the meaning of canopy. Indeed,
the hat in the portrait serves this latter function. Since
standing or walking under a canopy was one of the
privileges of princes, the title may indicate a subtle flat-
tery. It could, however, also contain a reference to the
canopy of marriage ceremonies. Rubens' model was
Susanne Fourment, who married (for a second time) in
1622. The painting could very well date from this period, when she was twenty-three.

It is easy to see that Rubens painted this portrait *con
amore*. The billowing forms of the costume, neutral in
tone save for one strong red, emphasize the smooth,
luminous, subtly shaded colors of the flesh. The blue sky
lends outdoor freshness, rendering all the more attrac-
tive the young lady whose pose is so modest and whose
expression is so alluring.

Rubens painted Susanne's portrait more than once,
and after the death of his first wife he married her
younger sister, the sixteen-year-old Helene Fourment.

Plate 13. THE GARDEN OF LOVE

(commentary follows color plate section)

PLATE 14

THE LANDING OF
MARIE DE MEDICIS

Painted 1622–23. 25¼ x 19¾"
Neue Staatsgalerie, Munich

Between 1622 and 1625, Rubens decorated the Luxembourg Palace in Paris with twenty-two huge paintings
(now in the Louvre) in honor of Marie de Medicis, the
French Queen Mother. A few of the many preliminary
drawings and studies have been preserved, among them
a series of color sketches in Munich from which our
plate has been taken. The painting shows the arrival at
Marseilles of the young Italian princess, who when still
a child had been engaged to the French king. As the fu-
ture queen of France moves forward, she receives a wel-
come typical of the age that exalted monarchs into
demigods. France herself, in the form of a helmeted
woman, greets her with outstretched arms. Overhead,
winged Fame spreads the message of her arrival. Deities
of the water appear like the foaming crests of surf,
eager to hold and make fast the ship. Thus, allegory
and mythology are called upon to join in the glorifica-
tion of the ruler.

Many a lesser artist, charged with similar tasks, has
lost himself in pomposity and dry learning. Rubens was
able to make strange happenings believable, tie together
old elements, and give to all figures such vigorous reality
that we accept them without question or astonishment.

PLATE 15

MARIE DE MEDICIS

Painted about 1622–25. 51¼ x 42½"
The Prado, Madrid

In the Munich sketch (preceding plate) and the corre-
sponding painting in the Louvre, Marie de Medicis appears as a young princess. How Rubens saw her when
he was working on the big cycle of her life we know best
from this impressive portrait which, though apparently
never finished, is one of Rubens' finest. He fully ex-
ploited in it the current fashion of his time for lending
majesty to figures by expanding them laterally. The huge
collar with its thin radiating lines provides a fine foil for
Marie's head and full neck. Still greater width is pro-
vided by the puffed-out sleeves and the enormous skirt.
The warm tonal areas of head and hands stand out strik-
ingly from the blacks and whites of the costume. The
masses of material and the hugeness of the shapes do
not interfere with a basic quality of Rubens' art—the
suggestion of movement. On closer inspection, the black
of the gown is seen to be full of life in form and color.
The undulating scallops of the cuffs and the collar contrast vividly with the more severe outlines of the dress
and the chair.

Rubens' sympathetic portrayal does not quite agree
with what history records of Marie de Medicis. His art,
like the sun, made bright and noble whatever it touched.

PLATE 16

THE CONVERSION OF SAINT BAVO

Painted 1612. 41½ x 65½"
National Gallery, London

This unusually elaborate sketch was made for a large triptych contemplated for the Cathedral of Saint Bavo in Ghent, but never executed in this form. The legend of Saint Bavo tells of a Count Allowin who upon conversion took a new name and gave away his fortune to be distributed as charity by the Church. In Rubens' plan, the main action was reserved for the central panel, with subsidiary parts of the legend appearing on the narrower side-pieces. The layout of the stage, with its various platforms and wide staircase, and the distribution and movement of the figures are designed to lead up to the dramatic meeting of the Bishop and Count Allowin. All the figures, however, are subordinated to the magnificent architecture, the true symbol of the power of the Church.

The Conversion of Saint Bavo, if finished, would have been one of the first and one of the greatest manifestations of Rubens' decorative talent. The sketch alone fills the eye with an almost overwhelming spectacle of color and forms in motion. At the same time, it is a work of carefully balanced relationships, for even in his grandest conceptions Rubens never forgot—and never betrayed—his classical heritage.

PLATE 17

THE ARTIST'S SONS,
ALBERT AND NICOLAS

Painted 1624–25. 62¼ x 32¼"
National Gallery, London (Liechtenstein Loan Coll.)

The portrait of his sons tells us a great deal about Rubens' social standing. The two boys are in elaborate costumes of fine materials, while the imposing architecture suggests a truly palatial home.

Not so long before Rubens, children's portraits were distinguished from those of their elders by little more than blander faces. Here we have no solemn puppets, but real boys with rosy cheeks and solid Flemish bodies. Each one is recognizable as a person in his own right. Albert, the older one, perhaps ten or eleven, is acting the little gentleman, complete with hat, loose glove, and elegant crossing of legs. The book that he holds in his right hand hints at a careful education (which, as we know, had been entrusted to one of Antwerp's foremost scholars). His younger brother Nicolas, about six or seven years old, watches with the frowning concentration of small children the helpless flutter of his live toy —a little bird to whose leg a string has been attached.

Rubens' first-born child, Clara Serena, had died in 1623, at the age of twelve. It was probably soon after her death that Rubens decided to paint his sons; the loss of one child may have made the portrayal of the surviving ones all the more meaningful.

PLATE 18

ADAM AND EVE

Painted 1628–29. 93¼ x 72½"
The Prado, Madrid

From early September, 1628, until the end of April, 1629, Rubens was in Madrid, where he had been sent as special envoy by Isabella, ruler of the Spanish Netherlands, to negotiate the conclusion of peace between Spain and England. In the royal palace he found the largest collection of Titians outside Italy. Although charged at once with painting portraits of the royal household and the court, Rubens, as we learn from his Spanish contemporary Pacheco, also made copies "of all the things by Titian which the King owns, such as the two *Baths of Diana*, the *Europa*, *Venus and Adonis*, *Venus and Cupido*, *Adam and Eve*, and others." All these copies he took back with him to Antwerp. After his death some of them were bought by the King of Spain, and today Rubens' *Adam and Eve* hangs in the same room with the Titian from which it was copied.

As a copy, it is rather free. Rubens introduced certain changes that stress the psychological relationship between the figures, and his picture is more densely filled than its prototype. We miss in Rubens' canvas the rhythmic grandeur of Titian's. We are rewarded instead with figures who look more natural, and whose drama, for that reason, seems more tense and touching.

Plate 19. LANDSCAPE WITH RAINBOW

(commentary follows color plate section)

PLATE 20

VENUS AND ADONIS

Detail of plate 4
Painted about 1635. 77½ × 95¼"
The Metropolitan Museum of Art, New York

The present painting was executed with all the technical brilliance of Rubens' last period. Accessories are done in free, spontaneous strokes, while the figures are smoothly modeled with translucent glazes. The colors form cheerful harmonies. The gleaming flesh-color of Venus and the red and tan of Adonis are surrounded by a festive orchestration of yellows and greens in the landscape, grays and blues in the dogs, blues and pinks in the sky.

The subject, however, is not gay. Adonis, loved by Venus, takes leave despite her warning pleas. With real feeling Rubens painted Venus' moist eyes, which try to absorb forever the familiar features, and her beautiful arms and hands which seem to caress while they restrain the hunter. The bodies of the lovers form an almost regular pyramid in the center of the picture. Yet there is no stability in this design. Strong diagonals, from the body of Venus to the raised arm of Adonis, and from the wooded knoll at the right to the open distance at the left, indicate that the youth will go where his sleek hounds are pointing, and where he will meet his fate. If Rubens avoided emphasizing the somber mood of the story it was, perhaps, because he knew that Adonis, after his death, was transformed into the beautiful anemone.

PLATE 21

THE ILDEFONSO ALTAR

Painted 1630–32. Oil on wood: central panel, 127⅝ x 92⅞"; wings, 127⅝ x 36⅛". Kunsthistorisches Museum, Vienna

Late in his career Rubens — like Renoir — turned to brighter color patterns. *The Ildefonso Altar,* with its cheerful dominant of pink over chords of white, light gray, light green, orange, and blue, is a good example. It was painted at the request of Archduchess Isabella, daughter of Philip II of Spain and widowed Governess of the Netherlands. Rubens had long served her loyally as artist, counselor, and ambassador. *The Ildefonso Altar,* the crowning ornament of this association, is also its swan song, for Isabella died soon after its completion.

The altarpiece originally decorated a chapel of the Brotherhood of St. Ildefonso in a church in Brussels. In the center the Virgin, accompanied by angels and four holy women, hands a chasuble to St. Ildefonso as sign of her favor. The light which bursts into the scene from above vouches for the supernatural character of the event.

Isabella and her husband Albert, splendidly robed and accompanied by patron saints, watch from the wings. At the time the painting was made, Albert had been dead for many years, and Isabella invariably wore a nun's black. Thus the picture, which has a miracle for its central theme, shows another on its wings. The artist's imagery has evoked a happier time, long past, and transfixed it in effigy forever.

PLATE 22

THE HOLY FAMILY UNDER THE APPLE TREE

Painted 1630–32. Oil on wood, 128 x 91¾"
Kunsthistorisches Museum, Vienna

This painting originally formed the reverse of the wings of the Ildefonso triptych (preceding plate), but in the eighteenth century these side panels were split and their outer surfaces joined to form an independent picture. In the shade of an old apple tree laden with ripe fruit two families meet. On the right St. Joseph accompanies the Virgin, who holds the Infant Jesus in her arms as she looks tenderly at the little St. John. His mother Elizabeth kneels and gazes affectionately at the Christ Child, while Zacharias, standing behind her, gravely offers the Child some apples plucked from the tree. For the seventeenth-century observer, this scene must immediately have recalled another occasion on which one person offered another the fruit of a tree. By accepting the apple, symbol of the fall of man, the Infant Christ acknowledges his mission of redemption and gives promise of ultimate salvation from the dour consequences of that fall.

Although charged with theological meaning, the scene has the charm of a rustic idyl. The symbolic lamb that follows St. John, and the burrowing rabbit opposite, seem fitting elements of the countryside. All the bright colors that occur throughout the picture are concentrated in the gay, cheerful apples. Even the angels who endow the tree with special significance seem like luscious fruit amidst its foliage.

(commentary follows color plate section)

Plate 23. DIANA AND CALLISTO

PLATE 24

THE THREE GRACES

Painted about 1636–40. 87 x 72"
The Prado, Madrid

Some years ago, a writer described one of Rubens' nudes as a portrait of "a woman who had taken no exercise." For anyone applying such standards, *The Three Graces* must be a hard work to appreciate. If any of Rubens' pictures is a touchstone by which to test the degree of one's understanding of his art, it is this panel of three life-size nudes. Even for Rubens' time, it was a bold piece. The goddesses of beauty and gratitude had been painted before, but never on such a scale and in such emphatic nakedness.

Objects such as a fountain, a garland, draperies, trees, and plants create a protective frame for the women, so that in spite of the long vista behind them they seem to meet in privacy. The brush which so lightly sketched foliage, water, and the laces of the white shirt seems fairly to have caressed the human form. A good deal of thought must have gone into the interweaving of the arms, the placing of the feet, the meanderings of the veil which unites the figures. Yet it is the beauty of the hair, the delicious freshness of the skin, the touches of translucent yellow, pink, rose, and a whispered blue, which make the exploration of this painting a constant pleasure.

PLATE 25

THE JUDGMENT OF PARIS

Painted about 1637-38. 78⅜ x 149¼"
The Prado, Madrid

The most celebrated of all beauty contests was one of
Rubens' favorite themes. In this, his last version, he
showed Paris thoughtfully pondering who should re-
ceive the golden apple which sparkles in Mercury's
raised hand. Paris' pleasant dilemma was made more
difficult by the bribes offered to him by the contestants.
Minerva, divested of her armor and accompanied by a
balefully glaring owl, promised military fame; Juno,
here shown with her proud peacock, offered a kingdom.
But Venus won the shepherd's vote by promising to help
him win the most beautiful of mortals as his wife.

Though not insensitive to either fame or power,
Rubens' own sympathies clearly lay with the goddess of
Love. While Minerva and Juno pirouette strenuously to
attract attention, Venus stands modestly between them.
In contrast to the impassive expression of the other contestants, her face derives its hypnotic force from an un-
disguised display of sensual enthusiasm.

The painting was bought by King Philip IV of Spain
on the recommendation of his brother, the Archduke
Ferdinand. The Spanish prince had asked Rubens to
modify "the excessive nakedness" of the goddesses, but
Rubens insisted that it was just the nudes which revealed
the boldness of his brush. Nor did it diminish the value
of the picture that Venus was—in Ferdinand's words—"a
very good likeness of the artist's own wife."

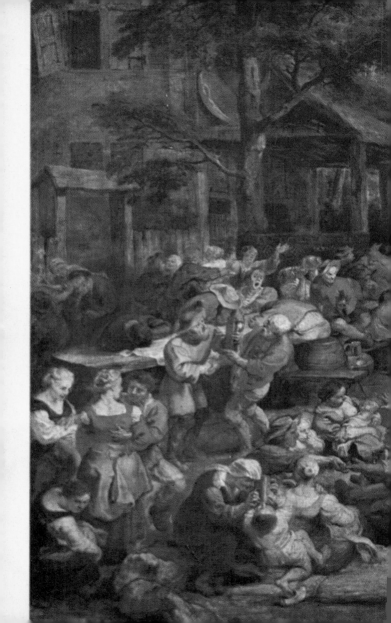

PLATE 27

CEPHALUS AND PROCRIS

Painted 1636. 11⅜ x 12⅝"
The Prado, Madrid

When he was nearly sixty, Rubens received a staggering commission. The King of Spain ordered him to furnish decorations quickly for his palatial hunting lodge outside Madrid. Within a few weeks, Rubens made sketches for more than sixty pictures and also painted a number of the large pieces himself. *Cephalus and Procris* is one of the sketches for this large undertaking. Like most of the others, it illustrates a fable from Ovid's *Metamorphoses.* A young couple were parted forever by the death of the wife, who was killed accidentally by her own husband. A report that on his hunting trips Cephalus could be heard talking tenderly to "Aura" (the refreshing breeze) made her fear that she had a rival. Driven by jealousy, she hid in the bushes. Hearing a slight rustle and suspecting the presence of game, Cephalus let fly his unerring javelin—a gift from Procris herself.

In Rubens' sketch, Cephalus turns his head in sudden alarm in the direction of the tree behind which Procris hides, her colors blending with the landscape. Tragedy is impending—but we still behold a bucolic scene. Rubens shows us the last moment which allows us to envision a happy ending. In the next, the fate of the unhappy couple will be inexorably sealed.

PLATE 26

THE KERMESSE

Painted about 1630–35. 58⅜ x 102¾"
The Louvre, Paris

The prominence that Bruegel had given to the category of "peasant painting" was not lost on Rubens, who always remained a Fleming at heart. Compared with Rubens' *Kermesse,* Bruegel's reveling peasants look static, immobile in picturesque silhouettes. In Rubens' painting, we feel almost as if the earth itself had come alive in all these rolling, swaying, turbulently active bodies. There is nothing here of the standardized choreography of a country square dance. We are closer to the orgiastic abandon of an ancient bacchanal.

All these figures, from suckling infant to tippling graybeard, are bursting with energy and are propelled by an irresistible need to convert this energy into action. Rubens has managed to give to the movement of these Flemish peasants something of the litheness of animals or primitive peoples. They belie the conventional statement that Rubens' figures are heavy. They may be buxom, but they are equipped with a wonderful muscular coordination and an elasticity strong enough to cope with their large bodies. If it were not for their costumes and their manners, they would remind us less of Bruegel's yokels than of the ideal types of Raphael and Michelangelo.

Plate 28. ALLEGORY OF WAR

(commentary follows color plate section)

PLATE 29

THE FUR CLOAK

Painted 1635–38. 69¼ x 38"
Kunsthistorisches Museum, Vienna

In his will, Rubens stipulated that the picture called *Het Pelsken* ("The Fur Cloak") should go to his widow. The painting shows Helene Fourment herself, nude save for the fur-lined and gold-braided mantle that she drapes almost diffidently around her body. It would be misinterpreting Rubens' intentions, however, to credit his decision to a desire to keep this intimate portrait from public view. There is evidence that it was well known. Rubens had every reason to be proud of this brilliant piece of painting, in which he had marshaled all his mature skill and tenderness to extol Helene's beauty. Her pearly white skin is made more glowing by contrast to the soft, dark mantle. Helene appears triumphantly, like Aphrodite herself.

Indeed, Rubens probably painted this panel with the sanction of classical tradition. Renaissance and Baroque painting offer enough examples of "Aphrodite Coming from the Bath"—derived from a prototype in Greek sculpture—to suggest that this was also the "theme" of *The Fur Cloak*. Yet Rubens has made it easy for us to forget the learned reference. His painting is less the image of Aphrodite in the borrowed features of Helene, than the image of Helene made so glorious as to encompass the idea of godlike beauty.

THE GARDEN OF LOVE

Painted 1632–34. 78 x 111⅜". The Prado, Madrid

Rubens' *Garden of Love* reflects the artist's happiness during his marriage to Hélène Fourment. Despite the contemporary costume, this is an allegory of love, related to a tradition which goes back to the Middle Ages and which finds its ultimate expression in the *fêtes galantes* of Watteau. The main theme is depicted with subtle variations. The couple at the right, with the woman leading the man, is balanced by the one at the left in which the girl still has to be persuaded and even needs a gentle push from one of the cupids. Two seated pairs are related to each other diagonally: one at the left faces out, the other, under the arch, turns inward. The central space is occupied by a man playing the lute, and by four young women, the target of the busy activity of most of the cupids, who hover near them or converge upon them from afar with various symbols of wedlock.

The fountain figure at the right is probably Venus herself, who all the while watches the central group with intense rapture. Looking at this figure, we sense that under the polite restraint of a *Conversation à la mode* there still run strongly some deeper emotional currents, such as found expression in ancient mystery cults and fertility rites.

LANDSCAPE WITH RAINBOW

Painted 1635–38. 53¼ x 92". The Wallace Collection, London

When the romantic painter turned to nature, he looked for solace and solitude. Rubens' landscapes, however, are the setting for many activities. Moreover, nature herself is "agitated" in his pictures. Wind and weather, light and shadow play across the fertile fields, the brooks and ponds, the grasses and the trees.

The landscape in The Wallace Collection is a good example of this approach. From its broad expanse there rises a warming sensation of contentment and well-being. A brief summer rain has cleared the air, and the sweeping embrace of a glittering rainbow reaches from one side of the picture to the other. Man and beast follow their normal tasks and inclinations. The sociable farm hands at the left, the cattle in the center, the preening and fluttering ducks at the right give life to each section of the picture. A few gay touches of red, blue, and white enliven the prevailing ochers of the fields and the greens of the trees. Deeply religious, Rubens saw in nature the work of God and communicates to us the joy with which he beheld creation.

COMMENTARY FOR COLOR PLATE 23

DIANA AND CALLISTO

Painted 1636–40. 79½ x 127⅛". The Prado, Madrid

Few pictures could be more symptomatic of the profound influence that Titian had on the late works of Rubens than this *Diana and Callisto*. Titianesque is the subdued harmony of color and the luminous treatment of human flesh. Moreover, the theme had been treated twice by the Venetian master, and Rubens clearly took from those paintings some ideas for his composition.

Callisto, one of Diana's chaste followers, was ravished by Jupiter in the guise of Diana herself. Her pregnancy was discovered when she refused to undress for a bath with the other nymphs. She was excluded from Diana's company and, after giving birth to a son, was transformed by jealous Juno into a bear. Years later, when her own son gave chase, Jupiter translated them both into the sky as constellations.

In Titian's painting, Diana dominates the scene. In a realm in which chastity is the highest virtue, the unhappy Callisto is clearly an outcast. In Rubens' version, Callisto, by far the most beautiful figure in the painting, appears to be the true heroine. The light which reveals her guilt also lends her a special, almost spiritual, radiance. This might well be Rubens' way of pointing out that Callisto, standing amidst the horrified nymphs of chaste Diana, was what they would never be—an expectant mother.

ALLEGORY OF WAR

Painted about 1637. 81⅛ x 134⅝". Pitti Palace, Florence

We are fortunate in having Rubens' own explanation of the *Allegory of War* in a letter that he sent in 1638 to Florence, where the picture had been shipped shortly before:

"The principal figure is Mars who has left the temple of Janus open (which according to Roman custom remained closed in time of peace) and struts with his shield and his bloodstained sword, threatening all peoples with disaster; he pays little attention to Venus, his lady, who, surrounded by her little love-gods, tries in vain to hold him back with caresses and embraces. On the opposite side, Mars is pulled forward by the Fury Alecto with a torch in her hand. There are also monsters signifying plague and famine, the inseparable companions of war. Thrown to the ground is a woman with a broken lute, as a symbol that harmony cannot exist beside the discord of war; likewise a mother with a child in her arms indicates that fertility, procreation, and tenderness are opposed by war, which breaks into and destroys everything. There is furthermore an architect fallen backwards, with his tools in his hands, to express the idea that what is built in peace for the benefit and ornament of cities is laid in ruin and razed by the forces of arms. I believe, if I remember rightly, that you will also find on the ground, beneath the feet of Mars, a book and a drawing on paper, to indicate that he tramples on literature and other refinements. . . . The sorrowing woman, however, clothed in black with a torn veil, and deprived of all her jewels and ornaments is unhappy Europe which for so many years has suffered pillage, degradation, and misery affecting all of us so deeply that it is useless to say more about them. Her symbol is the globe with a cross on top, which is carried by a small angel or Genius, the sign of the Christian world."

Plate 30. STUDY FOR "DANIEL IN THE LION'S DEN." 1614–17
Black crayon, 19⅞ x 11⅞". The Pierpont Morgan Library, N.Y.

Plate 31. THE LION HUNT. *1620-22. Oil,* 96⅞ x 147¼".

Neue Staatsgalerie, Munich

Plate 32. ISABELLA BRANT. *1625. Black and red crayon heightened with white, 15 x 11½". British Museum, London*

Plate 33. RUBENS' SON, NICOLAS. *About 1625. Black chalk heightened with white, 9⅛ x 7⅛". Albertina, Vienna*

Plate 34. FRANCISCAN ALLEGORY. *About 1635. Oil sketch for engraving*

Plate 35. HELENE FOURMENT. *About 1630–31. Black and red crayon heightened with white, 19⅜ x 12⅝". Boymans Museum, Rotterdam*

© ACL. Brussels

Plate 36. RUBENS' DAUGHTER, ISABELLE HELENE. *About 1636–37*
Black and red chalk, 16⅛ x 11⅜". The Louvre, Paris

Plate 37. WISDOM CONQUERING ENVY. *About 1630–32*
Oil sketch, 25⅝ x 20¼". Royal Museum, Antwerp

Plate 38. ST. CATHERINE. *About 1620–25. Etching,* 11½ x 7½"
The Metropolitan Museum of Art, New York

BIOGRAPHICAL NOTES

1577 Peter Paul Rubens born of Flemish parentage June 28th at Siegen, Westphalia.

1598 Accepted as master in the painter's Guild of St. Luke in Antwerp.

1600–08 Visits to Italy and Spain: works chiefly in Mantua, Rome, and Genoa.

1608–09 Settles in Antwerp. Appointed Court Painter. Marries Isabella Brant.

1610–20 Major commissions for churches in Antwerp.

1622–25 Decorations for Luxembourg Palace, Paris.

1626 Isabella dies leaving two sons, Albert and Nicolas. Rubens sells his art collection to the Duke of Buckingham.

1628–30 Diplomatic missions to Spain and England, where he is knighted by Charles I.

1630 Marries sixteen-year-old Hélène Fourment, who will bear him five children.

1633–35 Executes decorations in London, Antwerp.

1635 Buys the Castle of Steen.

1636–39 Works on the decoration of the Torre de la Parada near Madrid and other projects of King Philip IV.

1640 Dies May 30th in Antwerp.